THE
PSYCHOLOGIZING
OF
THE FAITH
BY BOB HOEKSTRA

PO Box 8000 Costa Mesa CA 92628

Published by **The Word For Today**
P.O. Box 8000 Costa Mesa CA 92628
ISBN 0-936728-56-6

Table of Contents

Preface

When Luke wrote the message of the gospel to Theophilus, he declared that his desire was to set forth in order a declaration of those things that are most surely believed among us. Luke desired that Theophilus might know the certainty of those things in which he had been instructed.

We seem to be living in a day of spiritual confusion. Paul wrote to the Ephesians that they not be as children tossed to and fro with every wind of doctrine by the slight of men and the cunning craftiness whereby they lie in wait to deceive. Because of all the confusion in the church today, and the many winds of doctrine that continue to blow through the body of Christ, we felt that it would be good to have various pastors write booklets that would address the issues and give to you the solid biblical basis of what we believe and why we believe it.

Our purpose is that the spiritual house that you build will be set upon the solid foundation of the eternal Word of God, thus we know that it can withstand the fiercest storms.

Pastor Chuck Smith
Calvary Chapel of Costa Mesa, California

Introduction:
The Redefining Process

A subtle and deadly process is at work in the church today in which the Christian faith is being "psychologized." This word speaks of the redefining of the Christian faith by the intrusion of psychological thinking into the church of the Lord Jesus Christ. It is related to secularism and humanism running rampant in much of the world over recent decades. The secularists are attempting to remove God from our thinking and our values. The humanists are at the same time trying to establish man as the source of all values and all necessary adequacy. These perspectives on life have helped establish psychology as a cultural religion for multitudes of people.

Many people would view psychology's influential position as an inevitable result of living in an enlightened scientific age. However, only a minor portion of psychological theory is capable of scientific verification (ie, whereby repeated experiments will always give the same results, thus indicating factors that God built into creation as He made it). Actually, the overwhelming portion of psychological theory is philosophical in nature. Psychology happens to be a way to view life. It amounts to an attempt to explain man (who he is, why he is here, how to develop him, how to solve his problems, how to meet his needs, and how to help him get where he thinks he needs to go). It is a philosophy of life with man at the center and with man as his own basic hope. Colossians 2:8 gives a strong warning about the philosophies of man. We will examine this warning in the concluding chapter.

Along with all of these developments in the thinking of the world, the church has for decades been weakening in its calling to be salt and light in the world. Consequently, instead of us affecting the world as we are supposed to be doing, the world is affecting the church. Instead of the people of God telling the world about Him and about His ways in all things, the world is now teaching the church the ways of man, as worldly thinking makes increasing inroads into the church.

This process is bringing us a new vocabulary and a new way of thinking about God and man. Actually, this means we are being given a new theology that is in conformity to this world. In this worldly theology, the Word of God is not forsaken all together. However, the scriptures get twisted and tortured in order to protect and propagate this new message. Foundational elements of "the faith, once and for all, delivered to the saints" (Jude 3) are given a new, popular, earthbound, psychological meaning. Many of us believers are convinced that the church desperately needs a warning call to come back to the Lord and to His Word.

The following consideration of various foundational truths and basic spiritual realities of life in Christ will demonstrate how the Christian faith is being given a new, worldly, unbiblical understanding. Our approach will be to look first at the Word of

God to define each given issue. Then, by developing sections entitled "Instead", we will consider psychologized perspectives that are being brought into the church world through Christian books, Christian radio, Christian television, and even through seminaries and Bible colleges.

Chapter 1
The Ministry of Counseling

Although the counseling ministry is not the most vital matter we are going to look at, it is both an important issue as well as an arena which is clearly and heavily impacted by psychological influence.

The Word of God declares, and our lives illustrate the fact that every Christian needs counseling regularly. This does not mean that we should seek or do seek an appointment with some professional counselor. It merely means that we need the direction of God time and time again. We are sheep who must have a shepherd to guide us through life, with all of its dangers and dilemmas (see Isaiah 53 and John 10).

God's Word also reveals that every Christian is responsible to give counseling to others periodically. This truth can be seen in Romans 15:14 and Colossians 3:16, where the term "admonishing" can be rendered "counseling." We are to be "counseling one another." Counseling is one of the many strategic "one another" ministries in the family of God whereby we each serve the other in a mutual and reciprocal way (as in Galatians 6:1, Ephesians 4:32, Hebrews 10:24-25).

The Lord as Counselor

The heart of the counseling ministry lies elsewhere. Isaiah 9:6 points us in that direction: "For unto us a Child is born, unto us a Son is given; and the government will be upon His shoulder. And His name will be called Wonderful, Counselor...." This Child to be born, this Son to be given would be the Son of God come as a man. This would be God in the flesh. The authority and responsibility to rule the kingdom of God would be upon His shoulders. Now, Christians know that this is the Lord Jesus Christ. He is to rule over the lives of the people of God. He is to guide every issue of thought and life for us. Notice this title that declares one of the great ministries that Jesus is to have among His people. "His name shall be called Wonderful Counselor." From this prophetic word of the Old Testament to the declarations of the Gospels and Epistles of the New Testament, it is clear that Jesus Christ is to be our Wonderful Counselor. He generally uses us as His instruments as He gives His counsel. However, He is the Counselor. We are not really the counselors. The pastor is not the true counselor. The staff member is not the counselor. The experts of the world are certainly not the counselors. Jesus is the true Counselor for the body of Christ. Any Christians who are actually counseling well are doing such by passing on the counsel of the Lord Jesus. In fact, it is the Lord who is counseling right through their lives to the one who is seeking counseling. This is the fundamental truth in the matter of godly counseling. The Lord is the Counselor. He is a Wonderful Counselor.

All Treasures of Wisdom and Knowledge

Now, just how wonderful is Jesus as our Counselor? Can He handle the task fully? Does He have all that is necessary to thoroughly carry out this important responsibility? A powerful answer to these questions is found in Colossians 2:3, "In whom (in Christ) are hidden all the treasures of wisdom and knowledge." Knowledge and wisdom are generally what people are seeking when they look for counseling. They are needing to know more and/or how to properly use or implement what they already know. All of this wisdom and knowledge is available in the Lord Jesus. All of the necessary wisdom and knowledge that is needed for "life and godliness" (to borrow an important phrase from 2 Peter 1:3) is all found in Christ. Every heavenly treasure of knowledge and wisdom for man to live as he should is all hidden in our Lord. That is how wonderful He is as our Counselor!

However, we do well to remember that these treasures are hidden in Christ. They are not lying around to be automatically picked up at church meetings or in visits to Christian counseling clinics or from sessions of a recovery group or by reading the latest Christian self-help book. They are hidden in a Person. They are not hidden there so that we cannot find them. Rather, they are hidden there so that we will know where the one and only place is that we are to be looking. These treasures can only be found by seeking after the Lord Jesus, discovering the wonders of Him and His work on our behalf and His provisions for us. The Christian life is a relationship with the living God. In order to allow the Son of God to counsel us, we must be developing a growing relationship with Him. We will give more attention to this strategic issue later.

God's Word in Counseling

How do we dig into these heavenly treasures? How does the Lord get His wonderful counsel to us? Psalm 119:24, speaking of God's Word, tells us how. "Your testimonies are my delight and my counselors." God wants us to delight in His Word, to seek Him in His Word, and thereby let Him counsel us through His Word. As we eagerly dig into the Word of God, seeking after Him, His Holy Spirit brings forth the heavenly treasures of our Wonderful Counselor for our lives.

This is the ministry of counseling as designed by God. Now, what is going on instead in the church world?

Instead

Instead of the ministry of counseling being the Lord counseling us with His treasures of wisdom and knowledge through His Word, here is what is happening. When hurting or needy people seek help, their churches often refer them to the human experts of the world who have been trained in psychological theory. This new, predominant trend involves sending troubled folks to the Christian therapist or, more and more, to the Christian counseling clinic. The difficulty here is that these Christian counselors generally have been trained in the same psychological theories as the secular therapists of the world.

Such counselors may be well-meaning. They may have tender hearts of compassion with great desire to help people. They may even be spiritually gifted by God in the area of counseling. However, their approach to counseling typically involves integrating the human speculations of godless theoreticians like Sigmund Freud, Carl Jung, Abraham

Maslow, Erich Fromm, and others with the divine revelations of our Wonderful Counselor. Some of the larger churches even have their own psychologically educated therapists on staff. This is going on even though the very core of these theories is contrary to Christ and to His Word.

This is not to ignore that Freud, Jung and the rest were very brilliant human thinkers. Their observations of man and subsequent conclusions were ingenious and intriguing. However, they were guessing about invisible, internal matters that only God can see and explain. Furthermore, they were doing such from a philosophical perspective on life that purposely left God out of the equation. *Only* God can look on the heart of man, evaluate it, and supply the remedy for the needs of the heart.

Some believers may say at this point that they have received help from Christian psychological counselors. Well, this is certainly possible. Despite worldly training, if a counselor loves God, believes in prayer, uses the Word of God somewhat, and has godly compassion for the hurting and needy, then there are a number of avenues available for the Lord to work through in that situation. However, this does not condone the purposeful use of the humanistic approaches of man. We must not neglect the commands, provisions and warnings of God whenever we see the Lord mercifully working in less than ideal conditions. We may see Him working in a way that is an exception to His basic rule, as in Numbers 22:28-30, when He opened the mouth of a donkey to speak in human language. However, we must not turn that exception into a new rule for life and ministry.

Furthermore, the Lord wants us in all areas to grow in love and discernment, seeking to find His most excellent way in all things. "And this I pray, that your love may abound still more and more in knowledge and all discernment, that you may approve the things that are excellent...." (Philippians 1:9-10). The Lord wants us to be continually growing concerning the differences between the bad, good, better, and most excellent. He is always calling us to the more excellent way. Certainly, in the ministry of counseling, our Wonderful Counselor wants to call the church to His perfect ways instead of to the ways of man.

Chapter 2
The Problem of Sin

If the psychological influence of the world upon the church were limited only to the ministry of counseling, this would still be a very serious situation for the family of God to face. However, the psychologizing of the faith is consistently and increasingly reaching into far more foundational issues than counseling. One example of this can be seen in the problem of sin.

Missing the Mark and Falling Short

Romans 3:23 speaks of what this problem is and of how extensive it is. "For all have sinned and fall short of the glory of God." The word for sin here is "missing the mark." If God's holy standard were a target right in

front of our face, we could not hit it even if we
tried with all of our might. If the glorious
character of God (seen in His laws and
commandments) were a measuring rod
reaching from the earth to the highest point of
the heavens, could anyone measure up? The
law says, "You shall be <u>holy</u>, for I <u>the Lord</u>
your God am <u>holy</u>" (Leviticus 19:2 and <u>1 Peter
1:16</u>). To measure up we must be as holy as
God. We have all fallen dreadfully short on the
basis of our own righteousness. This is the
problem of sin. It is a universal problem. It
affects all who exist or have ever existed or
will yet exist.

The Consequences of Sin

<u>Romans 6:23</u> elaborates on this matter by
describing the drastic consequences of this sin
problem. "For <u>the wages of sin is</u> death." All of
us have <u>sinned</u>, and what we have earned
from our sinning are some very serious wages-
-death. This not only involves physical death,
but, far more critical, it involves spiritual
death. Alienation from God, relational
deadness toward God was what we earned
through our sin. On our own we could not
know the Lord, please Him, walk with Him or
serve Him. We were all "<u>dead in trespasses</u>

and <u>sins</u>." (Ephesians 2:1). If these consequences of sin are not properly taken care of by God's one and only remedy, we would have to stay forever in that dead, alienated condition, never able to fellowship with the Lord.

God's Gift of Life

God has a glorious solution, and it is given in the balance of Romans 6:23. "But <u>the gift of God</u> is <u>eternal life</u> in Christ Jesus our Lord." What we earn from God on even our best efforts is death, for all our own works of self-righteousness are polluted with sin. God is willing to give us as a gift that which we desperately needed, but could never acquire on our own, that is, eternal life. It is a living, lasting relationship with the one, true and living God. It comes only through the wondrous work of another, the Lord Jesus Christ. What a glorious gift we have in eternal life. What a costly work the Lord undertook on our behalf to provide this gift for us. Jesus went to the cross to pay the debt we owed for our sins. He died in our place, drinking the cup of sin and death that was our appropriate judgment, that the Father "might be just and <u>the justifier</u> of the one who has faith in Jesus"

(Romans 3:26). So, the holy justice of God is satisfied, and He is freely able to offer forgiveness of sins and life eternal to all who believe.

The Abundance of God's Grace

These rich gifts of God's grace, as His remedy for the problem of sin, are unfolded even more in the fifth chapter of Romans. Herein we see not only forgiveness and new life available through Christ, but also how His provision includes the resources of God for living a fruitful and victorious Christian life. "Therefore, just as through one man sin entered the world, and death through sin, and thus death spread to all men, because all sinned" (5:12). This verse is speaking of Adam's sin, which introduced into the family of man the devastations of sin (rebellion against God, going our way instead of His way). Then, along with that rebellion came the alienation and spiritual deadness toward God that we are now considering. This death was then passed on to all mankind generation by generation.

All of us who had only been born once (natural birth, through the family of Adam's race) had passed on to us the condition of Adam. We too were existing in sin and death. This death rules as a tyrant dictator over all who do not yet have a second birth (a supernatural birth into the family of God). "For if by the one man's offense death reigned through the one...." (5:17a). The deadness of sin rules over the lives of the unredeemed. It is evidenced by spiritual blindness, fear, pride, selfishness, deceit, prejudice, sensuality, jealousy, etc. Herein lies the explanation of why lives are so troubled, broken and bound. "Death reigned through the one."

Much More Than We Need

However, God's remedy in Christ is abundantly more than our sin problem in Adam. "Much more those who receive abundance of grace and of the gift of righteousness will reign in life through the One, Jesus Christ" (5:17b). We all start out in Adam, in all of his sin and death. The only hope available, and the only hope we will ever need for time and eternity, is to become one who is "in Christ" (like a branch is in a vine) by faith in Him. When we humbly repent of our way and call upon the Lord for cleansing and forgiveness, we receive the gift of His righteousness that we may stand accepted before a holy God. Though this is a glorious introduction to His grace, it is merely our first step into the abundance of His grace.

The abundance of grace in Christ makes it possible for us to "reign in life." Reigning in life is being a Christ-like overcomer. It is growing and maturing in the things of Christ. It is living above circumstances instead of under them. It involves walking increasingly in the liberty of the Lord instead of in the bondage of the world. It involves walking in the wholeness of Christ instead of in the brokenness of man, but it can only be done "through the One, Jesus Christ". Such cannot be produced in any way by the religious efforts of man, even the dedicated and zealous attempts of a serious Christian. It is only "through the One, Jesus Christ." Reigning in life comes from trusting in, depending on, abiding in, counting on the One who walked upon this earth and overcame the world, the flesh, and the devil. It comes from looking to the One who always did those things which were pleasing to the heavenly Father. Then, as we draw life and strength from Him, we become more and more those who display His love, joy, peace, longsuffering, kindness, goodness, faithfulness, gentleness, and self-control.

Such spiritual fruit comes from the grace of God at work in and through us, because it is the life of Christ flowing into and through those who do not deserve it, could never earn it and could never produce it on their own. That is what life in Christ is all about. Jesus came "full of grace and truth" (John 1:14). "And of His fullness we have all received, and grace for grace (or, grace upon grace)" (v.16). The true Christian life is by grace from the moment of new birth right on into eternity. Christian living involves one layer of grace upon another, upon another, upon another, etc. Oh, how we underestimate the overwhelming abundance of the grace of God. Every day is to be lived by the sustaining grace of God. Every step of progress and change into greater heights of new life in Christ is to be taken by the transforming grace of God. Only God's abundant grace can take people from death reigning over them, to them reigning in life.

The problem that man faces is sin. First, it is our own sin. Then, at times, it is the sins of others toward us, or the sins of the world that come hard against believers in Jesus. The basic problem of mankind is sin. The remedy of God for all sin is the abundance of His grace to forgive, sustain, set free, transform, make whole, mature, guide, and make us fruitful. This is one of the foundation stones of the faith that the church of the Lord Jesus Christ is to guard, stand upon, and proclaim.

Instead

What is going on in much of the church world today concerning the basic problem of man and God's basic remedy? Instead of sin, man's problems now are dysfunctionalism or co-dependency or victimization or various types of "non-physiological diseases and disorders." This sort of psychologized thinking in the church is redefining in new, inadequate, humanistic terms what man's problems are all about.

The concept of dysfunctionalism is a prime example. Man observes or learns of a troubled family, and decides to call it dysfunctional. That is, this family is not functioning in a manner that we or the participants would desire. In that sense, "all have dysfunctioned and have fallen short of their desired level of human functionality." We can understand where such a term comes from. It is describing some actuality in human experience. However, it is using the wrong standard, and it does not go deep enough in its analysis. As a standard, dysfunctionalism says that I cannot function in a manner that I desire, or others did not function toward me in a manner that I desired. The true standard is what God desires, and He says that "all have sinned and fall short of the glory of God."

Co-dependency also is inadequate as a diagnosis of man's problem. Certainly people can wrongly attempt to find meaning for their lives by becoming dependent upon helping others who are wrongly dependent upon drugs, alcohol or whatever. The problem is not that we are sacrificing for others, in fact, the Lord calls us to lay down our lives for one another (1 John 3:16). Jesus tells us that greatness in His kingdom is measured in servanthood (Matthew 20:25-28). The problem is that we either serve self, or we serve others out of self-interest. The remedy is to learn to

serve others by the grace of God and for the
glory of God.

Victimization is another insufficient term
that people often turn to in trying to
understand their deepest problems. It
explains, and often justifies, our short-comings
as being a consequence of wrongs done to us,
so we thereby find justification for our
condition and/or place blame on others. Sure,
everyone has been wrongly treated and has
wrongly treated others, but we cannot build a
relationship with God on the basis of "they all
made me this way ". Neither can we relate to
others on the basis of blame. The problems
that we can deal with before God are our own
wrongs against Him and against others. We
can find that His remedy is forgiveness,
cleansing, transformation and reconciliation
(between God and man).

Another psychologized evaluation of man's
need is seen in trying to turn every aspect of
sin and carnality into a disease or a disorder.
So we are now treating the disease of
alcoholism and the disorder of compulsive
eating, instead of dealing spiritually with the
sins of drunkenness and gluttony. The

scriptures do not deny that we can have physiological needs, like chemical imbalances. God's Word does not disallow medical treatment for physical problems, either, when they are actually present. However, this does not mean that we can turn the spiritual problem of sin into mental or emotional diseases, and then treat them by drugs and individual or group therapy.

The ultimate problem that man faces is sin. Only God can deal with sin. Sadly, the problem of sin is being psychologically redefined in many churches today.

Chapter 3
The Call to Discipleship

Another foundational truth that is being redefined by the psychological thinking that is coming into the church is the call to discipleship. We are all called to be disciples of the Lord Jesus. A disciple is a follower, one who follows a master and teacher. "And He said unto them, 'Follow Me, and I will make you fishers of men'" (Matthew 4:19). This call from Jesus shows the simplicity and the power of true discipleship. The simplicity is seen in the basic invitation. We are to concentrate on following the Lord. The power is contained in the promise that He gives: "I will make you...." As we follow Jesus, He is working in us, on us and with us to make of us what He wants us to be. He wants to use His disciples to reach out and touch other lives. The way He does this is by making us more and more like Himself. This great transforming work cannot be accomplished through any other person, philosophy, theory, system or movement. We cannot remake ourselves, nor can others do it for us. Only by following Jesus Christ can we be fashioned increasingly into His likeness and thereby become increasingly useful in His hands. So, Jesus calls us to be His disciples, to follow Him. Then, He goes to work in our lives and sends us out to call others to follow Him as well.

Our Basic Instruction

The primary, overall instruction of Jesus to His followers was, "Go therefore and make disciples of all the nations" (Matthew 28:19). The whole Christian life involves following the Lord and helping others to do the same. We are to go about in all the world making disciples, saying, "Come, follow Jesus Christ; and as you follow Him, He will be remaking you."

Discipleship is critical and basic to "the faith, once for all delivered to the saints."

(Jude 3). In Luke 9:23, the terms of discipleship are given: "He said to them all, If anyone desires to come after Me, let him deny himself, and take us his cross daily, and follow Me." If people want to follow the Lord, here is what is involved.

Denying Self

The first issue to face in discipleship is denying self, saying "no" to self. Self is our problem-- self-centeredness, self-righteousness, self-help, self-hope. Long ago God spoke of man's need regarding self, "All we like sheep have gone astray; we have turned every one to his own way" (Isaiah 53:6). If we want to follow Jesus, be His disciple, and if we want Him to be changing our life by our following Him, then we must deny self. Another way to speak of denying self is repentance. It is saying "my way is wrong Lord; only Your way is right."

Taking Up Our Cross

The second issue of discipleship is taking up our cross. Denying self even unto death is encompassed in taking up our cross. Verse 24 makes it clear that death to self is ultimately referred to here: "For whoever desires to save

his life will lose it; but whoever loses his life
for My sake will save it." Taking up our cross
involves putting our hope in the cross of Jesus
Christ, because it is the only cross that can
bring an end to the independent self-life. We
put our hope and trust in Jesus and His work
on the cross, and, as far as God is concerned,
the old self-life is crucified. We become one
who by faith is crucified and buried with
Jesus, and is then raised with Him to new life,
born again into a new dependent life in Christ.
We still must learn that "if you live according
to the flesh, you will die (that is, experience
spiritual deadness); but if by the Spirit you
put to death the deeds of the body, you will
live (that is, experience spiritual vitality)"
(Romans 8:13). We take up our cross; make
the cross of Christ our cross, cling to it, hope
in it as our only remedy for our sins.

A Daily Way of Life

Notice the next word, "daily." Denial of
self is not something we do just at initial
salvation. This describes the way of life for
disciples. Day-by-day it is 'no' to self, my will,
glory, plans, resources, and abilities. Day-by-
day the disciple clings by faith to the finished
work of the cross. Galatians 6:14 deals with

this matter: "But God forbid that I should boast except in the cross of our Lord Jesus Christ, by which the world has been crucified to me, and I to the world". Every day we put our hope in the cross as the only way out of this world and its sin, death and guilt. The only way out is through death, death with Christ on His cross.

Following Jesus

At this point, we might wonder what can be left, since we are called to say no to self and cling to a cross that can bring death to self. Actually, what is left is everything that our hearts yearn for, and all that God desires for us, and has fully provided for those who will come to Him. It is all found in the last three words of Jesus' statement: "And follow Me." We say no to self and take up our cross that we might follow Him. Then in Him we find everything we need, not only forgiveness, but wisdom, insight, knowledge, strength, transformation, sanctification, the hope of glorification, heaven some day, and fruitfulness now. All of this is found following the Lord Jesus Christ. The Christian life, the life of discipleship, is a resurrected life, which is found in a resurrected Lord, and is developed by following a resurrected Lord! Anything else is other than and less than what God calls us to in His Word.

Instead

Well, this is what the "faith, once for all delivered to the saints" says about discipleship. Instead, what is going on in the church world as the faith is being psychologized? Instead of calling people to deny self, the church now urges people to esteem self. Self-esteem, one of the great new doctrines of the world, has become the rage of many churches, leaders, and authors. The tragedy of this philosophy is that it undermines true discipleship. It would be tragic if self-esteem just missed the discipleship path by five or ten degrees. We would still be seriously off course. However, the situation is far worse than that. Denying self and esteeming self are two opposite directions. One is humility, and the other is pride. One is God's way, and the other is man's way. Maybe that is why there is less and less discipleship in many churches. Surely, the Lord wants to bring us back to His ways.

Some have asked, "What are we to have in place of self-esteem?" We could call it many things, but simply to keep the same phraseology, we can call it "Christ esteem." Self-esteem means to hold self in high regard. Following Jesus, we are to learn increasingly to hold Him in high regard. We are to get all caught up in His greatness, love, provision, mercy, goodness, power, and work on our behalf. Another way to say it is that we are to get all caught up in His sufficiency. That is our next fundamental issue of the faith to be considered.

Chapter 4
The Sufficiency of Christ

The sufficiency of Christ is another vital foundation stone of the faith that is being redefined. Colossians 2:9-10 proclaims this marvelous truth about our Lord: "For in Him dwells all the fullness of the Godhead bodily; and you are complete in Him".

Completeness in Christ

All that God is and has for man, from heaven above, for life here on earth now, is available in Jesus Christ. "All the fullness" is in Him, and in Him every believer in Jesus Christ is complete. Notice the present tense is used, specifying a current condition. In Him you are "complete." You may say, "You certainly don't know me very well, if you think

I am a whole, complete person." No, it isn't a matter of us knowing each other. It is a matter of us knowing Christ. It is "in Him" that we are complete. It is the sufficiency of Christ, and the fact the He has fullness of life, that brings us completeness. His fullness and completeness are what we stand in for our acceptance in God's family. This very same sufficiency of His is what we hope in and draw on for our growth and effectiveness as God's children.

Christ, Our Life

Colossians 3:4 gives additional insight on our completeness in Christ: "When Christ who is our life appears...." Jesus Christ is coming back. That is our great and glorious hope. The point here for our study is this: Christ is our life. Christ not only gives us eternal life, but the life that He gives us is His life. To put it another way, the life that Christ gives to us when we believe on Him is His own life in which we are to share. The life that Jesus shares with us is the life that we are yearning to live!

We desire a life of love, peace, joy, goodness, kindness, faithfulness, meekness and self-control. That is what Jesus' life is like, and He is to be our life. Just as the life of a branch is not an independent life, but rather the life of the vine being shared, so it is with us and Christ. As Paul put it in Philippians 1:21 "To me to <u>live is Christ</u>...." This corresponds fully with the truth of "Christ is all and in all" (Colossians 3:11). Christ is to be our all-in-all. The plan of God is that the Lord Jesus Christ would live in all of His people and be our all to all of us.

Ministering His Life to One Another

What about our relationships with other Christians? Does not our need for them speak of some lack or insufficiency in Christ? Quite the contrary. The Lord has ordained that we should learn of Him and grow in Him as members of the body of Christ. Also, it is from His very fullness alone that we are able to minister to one another. Ephesians 4:16 and Colossians 2:19 both reveal that every member of the body of Christ is to hold fast to the Head, Jesus Christ, and then minister His fullness to one another, so that the body "grows with the increase that is from God." Life together as God's people is all related to the sufficiency of Christ.

Instead

The sufficiency of Christ is a foundation stone of the faith. However, we are hearing very little about it in the church today. Instead, we are hearing more and more about "how to" seminars on personal development. We hear about being all that we can be through our own best effort. We hear about self-improvement techniques and self-development courses and self-actualization principles and self-help literature and even self-help groups. What a different message this is from the sufficiency of Christ and all that He has provided for us and can do in and through us. The difference is between God's resources at work and man's resources.

How are we going to walk with God and serve Him and grow in Christ-likeness? Is it by the greatest development we can produce working on ourselves? Or are we going to draw on, tap into, count on, live by the sufficiency of the Lord Jesus Christ? He has a whole, complete life that is already ours, if we will just abide in Him, hope in Him, look to Him. The psychologizing of the faith is enticing people away from this full provision of God.

Chapter 5
The Sufficiency of God's Word

Our next vital foundation stone of the faith to be considered is the sufficiency of God's Word. This is emphatically stated in 2 Timothy 3:16-17 "All scripture is given by inspiration of God, and is profitable for doctrine, for reproof, for correction, for instruction in righteousness, that the man of God may be complete, thoroughly equipped for every good work." In these two verses there are three vital realities that convey the Bible's theology about itself: inspiration, authority and sufficiency.

Inspiration and Authority

"All scripture is given by inspiration of God" means that literally every word of the

Bible was breathed out by God through the lives of the apostles and prophets. Certainly, He used their vocabularies and their personalities. Nevertheless, He inspired every word. So every word is God speaking to man. That is why it is the faith once for all delivered to the saints. It is what God wanted to say to man.

These succeeding phrases indicate the authority that is inherent in all that He says. The Word of God "is profitable for doctrine, for reproof, for correction, for instruction in righteousness." The scriptures speak with divine authority in the realm of doctrine, that is teaching us about God and how to get on the path of discipleship and walk through life with Him. They also speak with authoritative reproof, that is telling us when we are straying from His path. Furthermore, they speak His word of correction, that is telling us what we must do to get back in line with His path of growth and service. They speak to us with instruction in righteousness, and that is how we can progress on down the path of His will for our lives. The Word of God, therefore, is comprehensively authoritative in our lives as well as being divinely inspired.

Sufficiency

There is another strategic biblical word here in addition to inspiration and authority. It is a critical one that is the focus of a real battleground in the church world today concerning the Word of God. The word is sufficiency. Verse 17 deals with this: " That the man of God may be complete, thoroughly equipped for every good work." Note the key terms that speak of the sufficiency of the word: complete, thoroughly equipped, every good work. The message of God's Word provides all we need for whole, complete lives in Christ. It can fully prepare us for every spiritual task that God has for us. This echoes the glorious truth we saw earlier in 2 Peter 1:3 that God "has given us everything pertaining to life and godliness, through the knowledge of Him." It is through the fully sufficient Word of God that we get to know our Lord and His complete provisions for us in Christ.

John 8:31-32 also gives great insight into the sufficiency of the Word of God. Jesus said to those who were believing in Him, "If you abide in My Word, you are My disciples indeed; and you shall know the truth, and the truth shall make you free." Real disciples live in the Word of God. This involves feeding on it and making decisions by it and trusting in it and obeying it. By so living in it, they get to know the truth of the Word. Then the truth of God's Word makes them free. There is such a great need in people's lives to be set free. So many things bind people. Fear, tradition, habits, confusion and so much more. God has a way to liberate us. It is through the truth of the Word of God. Oh, the liberating power of the Word of God. It is so sufficient.

John 17:17 gives another perspective on the sufficiency of the scriptures. Jesus is praying to His Heavenly Father: "Sanctify them by Your truth; Your Word is truth." He was praying for those who were following Him, and for all those who would follow through their testimony. So He is ultimately praying for all believers. The prayer of the Lord Jesus was that His followers would be sanctified, that is have their lives set apart from the world for the purposes, use and glory of God. Jesus revealed how this prayer was going to be answered. It would be by the power and effectiveness of the truth of God's Word. It alone is sufficient for the task.

God wants us declaring, living, believing, growing in, and passing on to one another this great foundation stone of the faith, the sufficiency of the Word of God. It is sufficient to make of our lives what God wants our lives to be: saved, sanctified, liberated, complete, fully equipped for service.

Instead

Instead, what is happening in the church world? Many, many churches no longer believe in the inspiration or authority of the Word of God, so they cannot be expected to proclaim its sufficiency. However, those churches that still hold to the inspiration and authority of the Word should also declare its total sufficiency. They too are now recanting by words or deeds the sufficiency of the Word of God. Even those in the church world who say we have the inspired and authoritative Word of God are teaching people to turn to the uninspired theoreticians of the world to get the final, sufficient answers for life. Those who have studied in the social sciences (or more accurately, the behavioral philosophies) are now viewed as those who have the sufficient answers for man.

The new creed in all of this is "all truth is
God's truth." It reasons that since God created
all things and since God is truth, any truth
found anywhere must have its source in God.
This thinking tends to place the discovered
truth of man (that is, human theories) on the
same level as the divinely inspired truth of
God's Word. Therefore, the message of a
psychological theorist out of the world can be
brought right into the ministry of the church
and integrated into the message for God's
people. This may be done by well-intended
church leaders, who want to help hurting and
needy people and assume that this is how to
do it. After all, these are the experts who have
studied man. They have the valid insights into
humanity. What happens in this process is we
end up greatly over-estimating man's wisdom,
while we tragically under-estimate God's
wisdom. The two end up on a common level,
and we grab a little bit of each, thinking we
are getting the best of all truth.

This "other truth" is man's best guess
about what is going on in an arena that he can
not really see: the heart, soul, mind and inner
man. Man cannot see in there. When he tries
to look in, he gets all confused, because the

heart is deceitful. God is the only one who can look upon it, and He is not guessing at what is taking place. He just looks in there, declares the way He made man, how man fell, what the resulting problems are, and what He has provided to make man whole inside. He has declared all of this to us in His Word. If we integrate human philosophies or theories into these matters of divine revelation, we are polluting God's truth. We are offering a new, psychologized faith to people for their lives and their walk with God. It is an undermining of the sufficiency of God's Word. This is a major aspect of the psychologizing of the Christian faith.

Chapter 6
The Work of the Holy Spirit

The work of the Holy Spirit is another basic, fundamental truth that is being redefined as psychological thinking that has come into the church. Jesus, speaking of the Holy Spirit in John 16:13-14, said, *"However when He, the Spirit of truth (literally, the truth), has come, He will guide you into all truth (literally, the truth); for He will not speak on his own authority, but whatever He hears He will speak; and He will tell you things to come. He will glorify Me, for He will take of what is Mine and declare it to you."*

Guiding Us into All the Truth

The Spirit of truth, the Holy Spirit, has been given to God's people to guide us into all the truth, that is all of the truth of the Word of God. This guiding ministry of the Spirit includes the studying and teaching of the Word of God right down through the centuries in the life of every Spirit-led child of God. In this process, the Holy Spirit focuses upon the wondrous realities of Jesus Christ and declares them to us. This function is one of the great ministries of the Holy Spirit. He has so many ministries. Here He glorifies the Lord Jesus by unfolding for us the riches in Christ available to us. Then, He gives us understanding of them, a heart to embrace them, and the motivation to walk in them.

Transforming Our Lives

2 Corinthians 3:18 speaks further of the work of the Holy Spirit: "But we all, with unveiled face, beholding as in a mirror the glory of the Lord, are being transformed into the same image from glory to glory, just as by the Spirit of the Lord." Consider what this verse reveals. It shows how lives are transformed into the image of Christ. Such transformation is what people need in their lives, but how could mere man with his theories, ideas and philosophies ever do this?

It is what God alone, by His Spirit, can provide.

The process God uses for transforming His people involves us coming humbly and openly to the Word of God. Then the glory of Jesus can be seen shining forth from the Word, as though reflected in a flawless mirror. The Spirit of the Lord uses that revelation of Christ to go to work in our lives, changing us into the same image, making us more and more like our Lord. The character of Christ has a life-changing impact on our character. We see more of who He is, and our hearts are molded and shaped in desire and direction. It is a progressive process from one aspect of His glorious being to another and from one degree of likeness to another.

We see an illustration of such change on a much lower plane in earthly, human affairs. People become like those to whom they give admiring attention. Or as God puts it in Psalm 115:8 concerning those who put their interest and allegiance in idols: "Those who make them will be like them, and so will all who trust in them." However, in the passage before us in 2 Corinthians 3, we are seeing the ultimate example of such influence by another. Here we see the Spirit of the Lord making God's people increasingly like Christ as they are continually exposed to the glory of the Lord Jesus!

These issues give us a brief look at some of the vital, irreplaceable works of the Holy Spirit. Such truth should be emphasized in our churches as another foundation stone of the faith.

Instead

Instead, what is being taught? Many leaders in the church say that life's problems are too complex today for these old fashioned approaches of the Bible and the Holy Spirit. Thereby, they are declaring the inadequacy of the Holy Spirit to meet the needs of people's lives or to accomplish the purposes of God. They thereby demonstrate their hope in intellectual answers instead of in spiritual answers. Much of the church world has opted so strongly for intellectualism. Not that God doesn't exercise our minds strongly. He says in Isaiah 1:18, "Come now, and let us reason together." God invites us to think with Him. It must be His thoughts that we are learning to

think, not man's. We do not imagine or
theorize the thoughts of God. He tells us of
them in His Word, and we think with Him.

On the other hand, the intellectual way is
the best that man's mental capacities can
produce. So, we end up trading off the power
of the Holy Spirit for the weakness of human
theories and philosophies. Remember, we are
called to a spiritual life in a spiritual kingdom.
Only the Holy Spirit can reveal spiritual
matters and make them real in our lives.
Actually, all of these theories of man out of the
behavioral philosophies represent man's best
attempt to help man become what man wants
to be, using man's own resources and his own
best effort. That is a world apart from "the
faith, once for all delivered to the saints". God
has His ways to make of us all that He wants
us to become. It is, "Not by might nor by power
(of man), but by My Spirit, says the Lord of
hosts" (Zechariah 4:6). We need the Holy
Spirit controlling our minds and revealing to
us "the mind of Christ" (1 Corinthians 2:16).

Chapter 7
The Supreme Goal of Knowing God

In Philippians 3:8, the Apostle Paul exclaimed, "Yet indeed I also count all things loss for the excellence of the knowledge of Christ Jesus my Lord." That could be rendered, "I count everything else worthless in view of the surpassing value of knowing Christ Jesus my Lord." The supreme goal of the Christian life of discipleship is aiming at the excellence, the surpassing value, that is knowing Christ. Getting acquainted with God is the ultimate issue of time and eternity.

Jesus put it this way in John 17:3, "And this is eternal life, that they may know You, the only true God, and Jesus Christ whom You have sent." That is why Paul could express his entire life's quest in one phrase, "that I may know Him" (Philippians 3:10). This was what he was speaking of in verse 13, when he described all of his life by saying, "this one thing I do." All of life is to be related to the supreme goal of getting to know the Lord more and more and more. Knowing God is the target at which we are to continually aim.

Multiplied Grace and Peace

Peter addressed this same issue in 2 Peter 1:2, "Grace and peace be multiplied to you in the knowledge of God and of Jesus our Lord." What would happen in our lives, if the grace and peace of God were multiplied toward us? Would that change our lives? Would that fill our lives? Would that transform our lives and equip us and enable us? Oh, this is what we need, God's grace and peace multiplied toward us. How do we enter into that? How do we avail ourselves of that potentiality? It takes place in the knowing of the Lord. A growing acquaintanceship with God unleashes His grace and peace in a multiplied way in our lives.

All that Pertains to Life and Godliness

Verse 3 elaborates on the significance of this growing relationship with God: "As His divine power has given to us all things that pertain to life and godliness, through the knowledge of Him." That is an amazing and glorious statement. God has exerted His power to make available to those who are in Christ Jesus all things that pertain to living life His way, as well as all that is necessary for growing in godliness. How do we avail ourselves of that wondrous provision? We increasingly enter into these realities through growing in knowing God. The more we get to know the Lord, the more we avail ourselves of all that He has provided for life and godliness. We thereby discover personally what His Word declares, that His provision includes everything that we need. This is a foundational truth of the faith.

Instead

What is happening in the churches in this arena as the faith is being psychologized? The new cry of the church is like that of the world; not to know God, but to know yourself. Instead of urging and assisting people along a path of knowing God, many are turning people to personal introspection through all kinds of sophisticated new "tools of ministry", as they are called. Self-evaluation tests and temperament analysis tests and personal preference inventories abound in the programs of the church. Though these tools may seem to bring much useful information, what we really need to know about ourselves is already revealed in the Word of God.

Those who are seeking to know God will learn His evaluation of man. His evaluation is what we ultimately must have, not only because it is the only reliable perspective, but also because it is a part of getting to know our Lord. So, "let us pursue the knowledge of the Lord (press on to know the Lord)" (Hosea 6:3). This pursuit is the supreme goal of life. As we are doing this, God Himself will be multiplying grace and peace in our lives, supplying unto us everything that pertains to life and godliness.

As the Christian faith is being psychologically redefined, the supreme goal of loving God is drastically changed. The same thing is happening to a related matter, which is the last issue that we will examine.

Chapter 8
The Great Commandment
to Love God

Let us look at one more fundamental issue
of the faith that is being redefined by
psychological thinking coming into the church-
-the great commandment to love God.

*"Then one of them, a lawyer, asked Him a
question, testing Him, and saying, 'Teacher,
which is the great commandment in the law?'
Jesus said to him, 'You shall love the Lord
your God with all your heart, with all your
soul, and with all your mind, this is the first
and great commandment. And the second is
like it , you shall love your neighbor as
yourself. On these two commandments hang*

*all the Law and the Prophets' " (Matthew
22:35-40).*

Two Comprehensive Commandments

The great commandment, the primary
instruction from God that we are to
concentrate upon, is loving the Lord our God
with all of our being. A second one is like it
which is also a love commandment. It
concerns giving loving attention to others the
way that we already do for ourselves. These
two commandments comprehensively
summarize all of the scriptures, because Jesus
added that on these two all of the Word of God
was hanging.

Men Loving Themselves

Now let's consider with these two
commands, a related word of warning. Then,
we will think together about what is
happening today in the church world on this
issue. The warning is from 2 Timothy 3:1-2
"But know this, that in the last days perilous
times will come; for men will be lovers of
themselves."

We are told here that the last days before
the Lord returns will be difficult and
dangerous days in which to live. The

difficulties are related to that which will characterize humanity in those days: "For men will be." Notice what is at the top of this startling, sobering list of characteristics in the last days: "Men will be lovers of themselves." This was given to the church of Jesus Christ as a warning, as something to be on the alert against and to avoid.

So these issues are to be a fundamental part of the message of the church. We are to be urging people to be giving the primary and major portion of their attention to loving God. Then they are to supernaturally give loving concern to others, just as they naturally attend to their own needs and interests. All the while they are to be careful to not get caught up in the last-days societal passion of self-love. This is basic to the Christian faith.

Instead

Instead of urging people to love God, to love others, and to be alert to the dangers of self-love, many churches now instruct people in what could be called the "self-love myth." That is the myth that we must learn to love ourselves first before we can learn to love others properly. Now how has this self-love

myth been brought into the church of the Lord
Jesus Christ? It has taken place by a blatant
adulterating of the Word of God. This is how it
generally happens: Church leaders read a
passage about these two love commandments.
Then, when they get to the end, they add
these scripture-twisting comments. "Now we
all know that we don't love ourselves the way
we should. So how can we ever love others
appropriately until we learn to love ourselves
first? And how can we expect to learn to love
God until we learn to love people the way we
should?"

Most people tend to affirm that statement
heartily. Many folks are periodically
discouraged or frequently disappointed or
somewhat disillusioned or heavily burdened or
haunted with a sense of failure.

When a church leader suggests that they
are really suffering from a lack of proper self-
love, they easily misread all of that emotional
load as an indicator that the leader is correct.
So they are fully open to the next steps in this
unbiblical reasoning. The resulting
implication is that we have to give time and
attention to learning to love ourselves

properly. This usually means that psychological therapy or a self-help recovery program will have to be undertaken, and another group of believers are off on a self-centered quest, perhaps hoping that someday they will master self-love enough that they can begin to learn to love others a bit. Then, maybe eventually, they can get around to learning to love God.

Now, why is that a twisting and an adulterating of the Word of God? For two basic reasons that come right from the very context of the central passage itself. First, this unbiblical teaching adds a third commandment. Second, the priority of the commandments is reversed.

Jesus said there are two commandments here, not three. In fact, He says that you can hang the whole Word of God on these two decrees to love God and love others. There is nothing left in the scriptures to hang on an imaginary third injunction pertaining to learning to love ourselves. Therefore, this false teaching is adding to the Word of God, which we are forbidden to do.

Next, and perhaps even worse, this
teaching not only adds a third commandment,
it reverses the priority. What did Jesus say is
the foremost command? Love God with all
your being. We must direct our main attention
here. Nevertheless, this new, twisted,
psychologized teaching says that we must give
our priority thinking to learning to love
ourselves. That is more than backwards, and
is becoming a prevailing exposition of this
passage in much of the church world today. It
can even be found in respected Bible believing
Christian colleges and seminaries. This is how
extensive the psychologizing of the faith has
become.

Chapter 9
Concluding Evaluation

In conclusion, let's allow the Lord to give us a few warnings and exhortations from His Word concerning this tragic development called the psychologizing of the faith.

Repeating Two Evils

God's rebuke to His people of old is so timely today: "For My people have committed two evils: they have forsaken Me, the fountain of living waters, and hewn themselves cisterns, broken cisterns that can hold no water" (Jeremiah 2:13). Many of the people of God today are in the process of repeating Israel's shocking sins of old. The true and living God had pledged to be to them their constant flowing supply of life and reality.

Instead of looking to the Lord alone to be and to provide all that they needed, they got involved in the religious systems of the world around them. How sad. How could they do this in light of all the Lord had done for them and had promised to them?

However, the church world is doing the same thing. Jesus Christ is our all-sufficient Lord, our life, our all in all, yet many are turning from Him to the broken cisterns of psychological theories.

These theories are clever and ingenious, but there are holes in their systems. They do not hold water. You cannot live by them, in the true sense of God's promised abundant life. So it all brings shame upon the name of our forsaken Lord as it brings spiritual deadness to His people.

Deceived by the Serpent's Craftiness

One of Paul's concerns for the early church was that she might be enticed to drift away from the God-ordained simplicity that pertains to Christ. His concern was related to the craftiness of our enemy: "But I fear, lest somehow, as the serpent deceived Eve by his craftiness, so your minds may be corrupted (or, led astray) from the simplicity that is in Christ" (2 Corinthians 11:3). In the garden, Eve succumbed to subtle trickery, not some obvious frontal attack on her relationship with God. By enticing the church to follow after psychological insights and theories, the enemy of our souls may have unleashed one of his craftiest tactics ever. It all sounds so scientific, so wise, so beneficial, so justifiable, so compatible with the things of Christ. It all appears to supply those contemporary perspectives and sophisticated remedies that modern man assumes are not available in the "ancient writings of the prophets and apostles". What could they know about dysfunctionalism or co-dependency or clinical depression or being an adult child of an alcoholic?

As I have shared studies like these in different parts of this country and overseas, some folks have challenged the simplicity of saying that in Christ, His Word, works and provisions to us, we have all that we need (that is, "all that pertains to life and godliness"). Remember, the danger facing the early church (and the church ever since) was that their minds would be corrupted and led astray from the simplicity that is in Christ.

Probably what people are afraid of are things that are simplistic, things that are so simple that there is no significant substance to them. The message of the Scriptures is that the whole kingdom of God is wrapped up in Jesus Christ. That is the simplicity. Follow Him, and He changes us! Follow Him, and all the fullness is in Him! Follow Him, and we are complete in Him! Follow Him, and find everything that pertains to life and godliness. Follow Christ, and we will grow in a fruitful, useful, purposeful life as we become instruments in the hands of Almighty God. It is all found in following Jesus. That is the simplicity, the lack of complication. However, it is not simplistic, in the sense of lacking sufficient substance.

If we think the simplicity in Christ indicates inadequacy on His part, then we greatly underestimate who He is and what He has done. If we told a fish that all it needed was simply the ocean, and the fish felt that we were being too simplistic, then we would know that the fish was unfamiliar with or was underestimating the resources of the ocean. Christ is far deeper than the deepest ocean. In fact, we are offered in the person and work of Jesus "the unsearchable (unfathomable) riches of Christ" (Ephesians 3:8). People saying that they need more than the simplicity of Christ is like a fish saying it needs more than the ocean!? The depths of the riches of Christ can never be exhausted or be shown as insufficient.

The Deceit and Futility of Human Philosophy

The previous section contained such a vital biblical warning concerning deceit that we should let the Lord emphasize it in another way. Colossians 2:8 gives us this additional viewpoint: "Beware, lest anyone cheat you (or, take you captive) through philosophy and empty deceit, according to the tradition of men, according to the basic principles of the world, and not according to Christ." We are to watch out for and sound the alarm about these perspectives on life. We are not to welcome them into the church. We are not to integrate them into our message and ministry. This certainly includes the psychological theories of man.

We must not allow anyone to lead us into these directions. This warning and prohibition applies no matter how well educated, intended, popular, or influential in the church a leader may be. Beware, lest anyone captivate your thinking through any of these matters. Philosophy is man's way of viewing man and life and how to help and/or change people. Empty deceit involves humanly contrived ways of thinking that originate in spiritual deception and therefore are not built upon true godly realities. The tradition of man is another area of dangerous enticement, because it is merely man passing on to man that which seemed to be useful or desirable. Closely related to these traditions are the basic principles of the world which represents the contemporary, conventional wisdom and accepted procedures of society.

Jesus said, "My kingdom is not of this world" (John 18:36). How can we mix the wisdom of the kingdom of man with the kingdom of God? God's pronouncement on the wisdom of this world is given in 1 Corinthians 3:19-20 "For the wisdom of this world is foolishness with God. For it is written, 'He catches the wise in their own craftiness'; and again, 'the Lord knows the thoughts of the wise, that they are futile'". God says man's wisdom is foolishness. All of these psychological theoreticians who have intrigued the church in our day seem so brilliant, when measured against other humans. However, before God, they are foolish, because they did not learn from God, but rather, from their own vain imaginations. Also the Lord is fully aware of the thoughts of the wise. He knows all about the theories of those who possess special measures of human genius, like Freud, Adler, Jung, Maslow, Fromm, Rogers, and on and on. He says their thoughts are futile. That word means useless, vain, empty. They are of no value to God in developing His kingdom and building the lives of His people. We must be watching out for anything that is not according to Christ. Only Jesus Christ and His ways and His truth are to be guiding and shaping our lives.

Proclaiming God's Word

With these warnings from God laid out before us, it is so clear that we must be proclaiming only the message of God's Word: *"Preach the Word! Be ready in season and out of season. Convince, rebuke, exhort, with all longsuffering and teaching. For the time will come when they will not endure sound doctrine, but according to their own desires, because they have itching ears, they will heap up for themselves teachers; and they will turn their ears away from the truth, and be turned aside to fables." (2 Timothy 4:2-4).*

We are called in the family of God to proclaim the Word of God, not man's theories. Included in this fundamental exhortation is a prophesy that the time was coming when people would not settle for sound doctrine. They would not be interested in healthy, life-giving, biblical teaching. Rather, they would desire to hear those things which pleased their flesh, even if it involved fables and myths and theories, instead of the truth. Surely these words speak of the days in which we live. Many church leaders are turning away from the truth to proclaim a message that is heavily integrated with mythic, humanistic, psychological concepts, which titillate fleshy ears. So many of God's people are crying out for more.

Guarding and Holding Fast to the Faith

God has entrusted into our care and use His Word, "the faith once for all delivered to the saints". We are to guard it by staying away from all of the human systems of philosophical knowledge. We are to adhere strongly to the exact pattern of spiritually healthy teaching given to us through the prophets and apostles in the scriptures. The Lord made this very clear in His message through Paul to Timothy: *"O Timothy! Guard what was committed to your trust, avoiding the profane and idle babblings and contradictions of what is falsely called knowledge; by professing it some have strayed concerning the faith.... Hold fast the pattern of sound words which you have heard from me, in faith and love which are in Christ Jesus. That good thing which was committed to you, keep by the Holy Spirit who dwells in us"* (1 Timothy 6:20-21 and 2 Timothy 1:13-14).

We must not do this in a self-righteous, know-it-all attitude. It must be done humbly in the love that is in Christ Jesus, but, it must be done. We must keep this good deposit of absolute, divine truth that has been given to us. However, we can only do it by the powerful

working of the Holy Spirit who lives in God's
people. This is another great, indispensable
ministry of the Spirit. The only way to guard
this treasure of the Word of God and keep it
pure in our lives, churches and ministries is
by giving ourselves to the guidance, teaching
and power of the Holy Spirit working in our
lives through the Word. No other approach
will stand up against the onslaught that is
trying to redefine the faith. He alone can give
us the insight, discernment, wisdom, courage,
alertness, and love that we need for this
critical task. He is fully able.

May the Spirit of the Lord give us eyes to
see what is happening in the psychologizing of
the faith. May He give us hearts to be
instruments in His work of spiritual
restoration. Amen.

Pastor Bob Hoekstra
P.O. Box 1200
Vista, CA 92085-1200

Phone: 1-619-630-4447
Fax: 1-619-630-8915